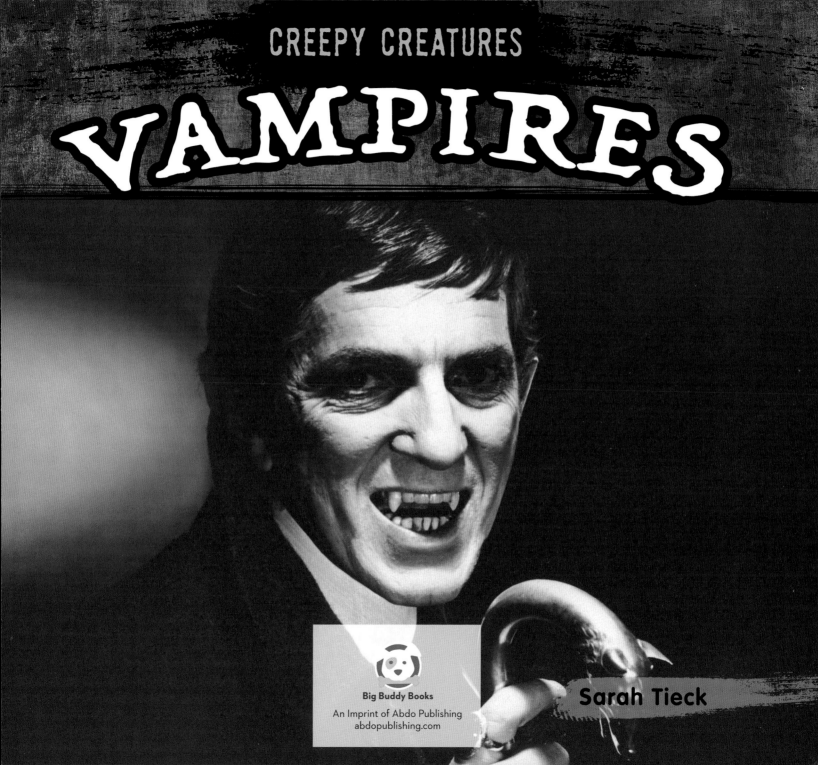

Creepy Creatures

VAMPIRES

Big Buddy Books
An Imprint of Abdo Publishing
abdopublishing.com

Sarah Tieck

abdopublishing.com

Published by Abdo Publishing, a division of ABDO, PO Box 398166, Minneapolis, Minnesota 55439.
Copyright © 2016 by Abdo Consulting Group, Inc. International copyrights reserved in all countries. No part
of this book may be reproduced in any form without written permission from the publisher. Big Buddy Books™
is a trademark and logo of Abdo Publishing.

Printed in the United States of America, North Mankato, Minnesota.
042015
092015

THIS BOOK CONTAINS
RECYCLED MATERIALS

Cover Photo: ABC Television/Getty Images.
Interior Photos: ASSOCIATED PRESS (pp. 19, 24, 25, 27); BAO/Glow Images (p. 13); Robert B. Fishman/
    picture-alliance/dpa/AP Images (p. 17); Getty Images (p. 25); Hulton Archive/Getty Images (pp. 5, 22);
    ©iStockphoto.com (pp. 9, 11, 21, 29); © North Wind Picture Archives (p. 15); Shutterstock.com
    (pp. 7, 23, 30); Silver Screen Collection/Getty Images (p. 7); Universal History Archive/Getty
    Images (p. 17).

Coordinating Series Editor: Rochelle Baltzer
Contributing Editors: Megan M. Gunderson, Bridget O'Brien, Marcia Zappa
Graphic Design: Jenny Christensen

Library of Congress Cataloging-in-Publication Data

Tieck, Sarah, 1976- author.
  Vampires / Sarah Tieck.
      pages cm. -- (Creepy creatures)
  ISBN 978-1-62403-767-2
  1. Vampires--Juvenile literature. I. Title.
  GR830.V3T54 2016
  398.21--dc23
                              2015004213

Contents

Creepy Vampires

People love to tell spooky stories, especially about creepy creatures such as vampires. They describe their sharp teeth. They say vampires come to life at night to drink blood.

Vampires have appeared in books, stories, plays, television shows, and movies. But are they real, or the stuff of **legend**? Let's find out more about vampires, and you can decide for yourself!

A famous vampire movie called *Nosferatu* came out in 1922. It features the creepy vampire Count Orlok (*right*).

Scary Stories

In stories, vampires are usually undead creatures that drink human blood. They have pale skin and **fangs**. They wear black.

Stories describe vampires as living alone. Vampires sleep during the day. At night, they rise from their coffins and go out to look for victims.

Did you know?

Vampire is also spelled *vampyre*.

In some stories, vampires sleep in coffins. Many are hundreds of years old!

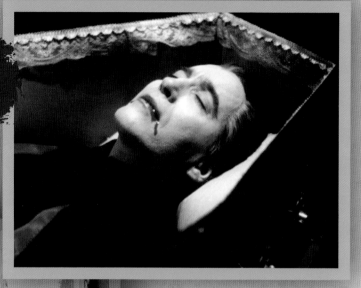

Vampires may not appear in pictures or mirrors. Some say this is because they don't have souls.

People become vampires in different ways. Often, a person is changed into a vampire by another vampire called a **sire**.

In many stories, vampires are very strong and fast. They can control people's minds. And, they can change form!

Yet, vampires do have weaknesses. They may burn up if they go outside in sunlight. And, they are **repelled** by garlic and Christian crosses. They can also be killed by a wooden stake through the heart.

Have you seen a bat fly through the night? Stories say vampires can change into bats!

Vampire Lore

Ancient Greeks told of people being attacked by creatures who took blood. These are the first known stories of vampire-like beings.

In **medieval** Europe, people told stories about dead bodies coming to life. They believed these undead creatures drank the blood of living people.

Did you know?

In some legends, a person becomes a vampire because of a vampire bite to the neck.

Blood is food for vampires. So, they bite people when they need to eat.

People's fears soon turned to real-life **hysteria**. They wanted to make sure the dead could not return.

People began burying bodies in certain ways so they could not become vampires. Some put a stake through the bodies. Others buried bodies upside down so the dead could not find their way out of their graves.

In Romania, people shot dead bodies because they were afraid the dead could come back.

Science Bite

Long ago, people didn't know as much about science as they do today. This caused misunderstanding and fear.

Certain illnesses caused **comas**. People thought their loved ones had died, but sometimes they woke up. This caused worry about the undead.

Bodies change after death. Living people saw the dead's nails and hair appear to grow. This added to the fear that bodies were not really dead.

In the past, many illnesses were misunderstood. Today, scientists can explain the things vampires are said to do. Certain sicknesses may cause people to bite, move away from garlic, and avoid light.

Around the World

People from many **cultures** tell vampire stories. Myths were especially popular in eastern Europe.

One famous story started in the 1400s. Prince Vlad III Dracula lived in Transylvania. This is in present-day Romania. He hurt many people.

Later, writer Bram Stoker read about this prince. It gave him the idea for *Dracula*, which is about a vampire. The modern idea of vampires comes from this book, which came out in 1897.

Bran Castle in Romania is popular with visitors. Many believe it looks like Dracula's castle in Bram Stoker's book.

Vlad III Dracula was also called Vlad the Impaler. People in Romania still tell stories of him.

People around the world continued to fear vampires. In the early 1900s, some Bulgarian villagers buried bodies they believed to be vampires. They buried the bodies with stakes through them.

Over the years, people have died from unusual bites or blood loss. This has happened in Africa and Europe as recently as the early 2000s. These deaths made some modern people believe vampires are real.

Graves containing bodies buried with stakes through them are called vampire graves.

Good or Evil?

In many stories, vampires are evil. They trick and kill people. People have to find ways to stay safe. Some become vampire hunters.

Yet in some stories, vampires are good. They drink the blood of animals instead of people. They use their strength to keep people safe. Some even use their powerful vampire blood to heal people.

Vampire hunters carry crosses, garlic, and stakes for protection against vampires.

Dracula

In 1897, Bram Stoker (*left*) wrote a book about a vampire named Dracula. Count Dracula was based on Vlad III Dracula. This book has inspired other works about the vampire, including many movies.

Vampires in Pop Culture

Count Chocula

This cartoon character appears on the front of the monster-themed cereal. Introduced in 1971, Count Chocula wears a cape and has pointed ears.

Edward Cullen

Edward is a main character in Stephenie Meyer's Twilight Saga books. Edward is not an evil vampire. He loves a human named Bella. In movies based on the books, he was played by Robert Pattinson.

The Count

This famous puppet helps children learn numbers on *Sesame Street*. He is a friendly vampire. He first appeared on the show in 1972.

Angel

This vampire appeared in *Buffy the Vampire Slayer* in the late 1990s. Unlike many vampires, he had a soul. Later, this character got his own TV show called *Angel*.

Fact or Fiction?

Many of the reasons people believed in vampires long ago came from sicknesses people did not understand. Today, scientists know a lot about human bodies. So now, most people don't believe vampires are real.

Yet vampires remain popular. Some are in action stories and comic books. Others are in scary movies and love stories. There are even events for fans of vampires.

The Twilight Saga books and movies gained millions of fans.

27

What Do You Think?

So, what do you think about vampires? Do they still send a chill up your spine? It can be fun to tell spooky vampire stories or to dress as vampires on Halloween.

It is also interesting to learn about vampires. Knowing what is true and what is made up is powerful. Read some vampire **fiction**, or discover the history that made people believe in them. You're in for an interesting journey!

People use fake teeth, face paint, and black clothes to dress up as vampires.

Let's Talk

What examples of vampires can you think of?

If you were a vampire hunter, what tools would you carry?

How do you think it would feel to live in a place where people believed there might be vampires?

If you were to write a story about a vampire, what sort of life would your vampire live?

Can you think of any other times where stories started because of real-life events?

Glossary

coma lack of consciousness, with loss of reaction to stimulus and spontaneous nervous activity.

culture (KUHL-chuhr) the arts, beliefs, and ways of life of a group of people.

fangs long, sharp teeth.

fiction stories that are not real.

hysteria a situation in which many people behave in an uncontrolled way because of fear or other strong feelings.

legend an old story that many believe, but cannot be proven true.

medieval relating to the period of European history from about AD 500 to about 1500. This time is also called the Middle Ages.

repel to push away.

sire someone that originates, or brings into being.

Websites

To learn more about Creepy Creatures, visit **booklinks.abdopublishing.com**. These links are routinely monitored and updated to provide the most current information available.

Index

31901059560070